D1545329

Joshua Wong
Student Activist for Democracy

Linda Barghoorn

Crabtree Publishing Company
www.crabtreebooks.com

Author: Linda Barghoorn

Series research and development: Reagan Miller

Editorial director: Kathy Middleton

Editor: Ellen Rodger

Proofreader: Wendy Scavuzzo

Photo researchers: Samara Parent and Ellen Rodger

Designer and prepress technician: Samara Parent

Print coordinator: Katherine Berti

Photographs:
AP Photo: © Kin Cheung: title page, pages 16, 28-29; © Vincent Yu: pages 4-5, 24-25, 27

Getty Images: © Dimitrios Kambouris: cover; © Lam Yik Fei/Bloomberg: pages 18, 22; © ANTHONY WALLACE/AFP: pages 23, 26

Shuttertstock.com: © Sorbis: page 6; © MADSOLAR: page 7; © Gwoeii: page 8 (top right); © TungCheung: page 10; © Matt Leung: pages 12-13; © Nattee Chalermtiragool: page 17; © Lewis Tse Pui Lung: page 19; © gary yim: page 21

Wikimedia Commons: © Voice of America: pages 11, 14, 15, 30; © Seader: page 20

All other images from Shutterstock

About the author: Linda Barghoorn has been sharing stories—hers and others—for years. She has interviewed rap musicians, TV news anchors, and most importantly, her dad. She is the author of several children's books and is working on a novel about her father's life.

Library and Archives Canada Cataloguing in Publication

Barghoorn, Linda, author
    Joshua Wong : student activist for democracy / Linda Barghoorn.

(Remarkable lives revealed)
Includes index.
Issued in print and electronic formats.
ISBN 978-0-7787-4874-8 (hardcover).--
ISBN 978-0-7787-4873-1 (softcover).--ISBN 978-1-4271-2100-4 (HTML)

    1. Huang, Zhifeng, 1996- --Juvenile literature. 2. Political activists--China--Hong Kong--Biography--Juvenile literature. 3. Student protesters--China--Hong Kong--Biography--Juvenile literature. 4. Social reformers--China--Hong Kong--Biography--Juvenile literature. 5. Protest movements--China--Hong Kong--Juvenile literature. 6. Hong Kong (China)--History--21st century--Juvenile literature. I. Title. II. Series: Remarkable lives revealed

DS796.H753H83 2018   j951.2506092   C2017-907732-5
                                                   C2017-907733-3

Library of Congress Cataloging-in-Publication Data

CIP available at the Library of Congress

Crabtree Publishing Company
www.crabtreebooks.com   1-800-387-7650

Printed in the U.S.A./032018/BG20180202

Published in Canada
Crabtree Publishing
616 Welland Ave.
St. Catharines, Ontario
L2M 5V6

Published inthe United States
Crabtree Publishing
PMB 59051
350 Fifth Ave., 59th Floor
New York, NY 10118

Published in theUnited Kingdom
Crabtree Publishing
Maritime House
Basin Road North, Hove
BN41 1WR

Published in Australia
Crabtree Publishing
3 Charles Street
Coburg North
VIC, 3058

Contents

Strength of Spirit

Each of us is shaped by our actions, as well as the challenges and triumphs we face. These experiences form our life story—a story that is unique to each person. By sharing our life stories, we learn what inspires or motivates others. Some people have remarkable stories of dedication, strength, or compassion. Their stories can encourage us to learn more about issues and take action to shape the world we live in.

What Is a Biography?

A biography is the story of a person's life and experiences. We read biographies to learn about another person's life and thoughts. Biographies can be based on many sources of information. Primary sources include a person's own words or pictures. Secondary sources come from friends, family, media, or research.

Joshua credits his parents with teaching him about justice and freedom.

Joshua Wong

Joshua Wong is a student **activist** from Hong Kong who is known for his fearlessness, determination, and strong sense of **social justice**. He has encouraged thousands of youth in Hong Kong to stand up for their beliefs. He leads the fight for **democracy**, freedom, and individual rights.

? THINK ABOUT IT

Do you know someone remarkable? What are some of the qualities that make them special?

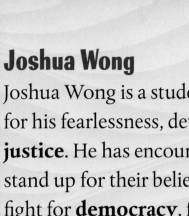

A Shaky Democracy

Joshua Wong Chi-fung was born in British-controlled Hong Kong on October 13, 1996. Nine months later, Hong Kong was returned to China by its British rulers. This event brought many changes to the lives of Hong Kong citizens. Raised as an only child in a middle-class family, Joshua was strongly influenced by his parents' values. His father Roger Wong was a Christian church **elder**. He often took Joshua to visit people who were less privileged. These visits revealed the **inequalities** that existed within society. Mr. Wong also shared stories and videos that showed how the Chinese government sometimes **repressed** its people, limiting their rights and freedoms. Joshua became aware of the social injustices that existed in China and its territory, Hong Kong.

The wealthy in Hong Kong can afford to buy goods in luxury brand stores.

A Passionate Speaker

As a teenager, Joshua became a passionate and eloquent speaker. He often tried to persuade others of the need for change, lecturing his classmates and even strangers. Joshua's father always encouraged him to be fearless in his determination to overcome obstacles in his life.

Some people can't afford housing in Hong Kong. They sleep on the streets.

The Face of a Movement

By the time he was 16, Joshua was leading a youth movement that challenged its government's policies on education and human rights. Small in size, he did not look like someone who could take on the giant task of fighting for democracy. But when he felt that Hong Kong's independence and his personal freedoms were at risk, Joshua knew he had to speak out.

> *Hong Kong is the place that I was born, I live, and the place that I love.*
>
> —*Joshua: Teenager vs. Superpower*, video, 2017

Hong Kong was ruled by Britain for 156 years. Queen Elizabeth II was shown on Hong Kong stamps until the territory was returned to China.

Understanding Hong Kong

To understand Joshua's activism, it's important to understand the city where he lives. Hong Kong is a tiny territory that was captured from China by the British in the 1800s. It grew wealthy under British rule, and became one of the world's leading financial centers. Under British rule, people often enjoyed more personal freedoms. Many had a better standard of living than those in neighboring China.

Hong Kong

Hong Kong is home to more than 7.4 million people. It is one of the most densely populated and expensive cities on Earth. It has a dramatic skyline with soaring skyscrapers, a wide harbor, and green mountains.

One Country, Two Systems

In 1984, China and Great Britain signed an agreement to return Hong Kong to Chinese rule. In China's **Communist** system, the government controls its economy, laws, and the rights of the people. The agreement promised to follow the "one country, two systems" principle. This meant that although Hong Kong and China would become one country, they would continue to have their own systems of government, economy, and law.

East Meets West

Hong Kong has been called the place "where east meets west." Although its heritage is Chinese, Hong Kong has many visible western influences as a former British colony.

State Control

In 1997, Hong Kong was returned to China. Today, while certain laws in Hong Kong protect individuals' rights and freedoms, Chinese law controls much of daily life in Hong Kong. As China exerted more influence over what was taught in Hong Kong schools and who could be elected to government, people worried about the loss of personal freedoms and independence. Joshua Wong and other critics argued that although Hong Kong had never had democracy, its laws were being changed to make it less free.

? THINK ABOUT IT

Why was Joshua worried about the future of freedom in Hong Kong?

The Making of an Activist

Joshua Wong began his activism career with a 2010 protest against a proposed railway line. The Chinese government planned to build a line connecting Guangzhou, China, with Hong Kong. Some Hong Kong residents opposed the idea. Joshua joined thousands of protestors who were worried about noise pollution and high costs.

Scholarism

The following year, Joshua and his classmate Ivan Lam created a student activist group called Scholarism. Joshua was only 14 years old. The group's first protest was against proposed changes to the government's school **curriculum**. They worried that China was interfering with the independence of Hong Kong's education system. They claimed the government in Beijing was trying to erase controversial historical events in China.

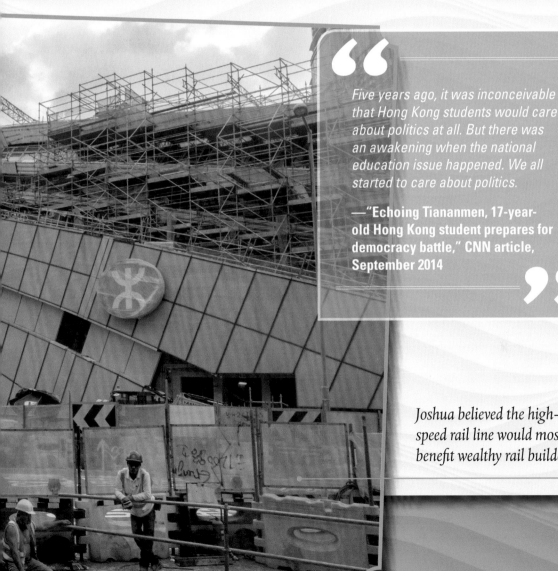

" Five years ago, it was inconceivable that Hong Kong students would care about politics at all. But there was an awakening when the national education issue happened. We all started to care about politics.

—"Echoing Tiananmen, 17-year-old Hong Kong student prepares for democracy battle," CNN article, September 2014 "

Joshua believed the high-speed rail line would mostly benefit wealthy rail builders.

Power and Influence

Membership in Scholarism grew quickly as students rallied together in protest. Joshua encouraged his fellow students to skip school and occupy the streets. Their September 2012 demonstration against the curriculum changes brought together more than 120,000 students and citizens. Under such enormous pressure, the government was forced to withdraw its proposed changes. Joshua began to understand the incredible power and influence of Hong Kong's youth activists.

Scholarism members meet in Hong Kong. They crossed their arms as a gesture of protest against changes to the school curriculum.

A Teenage Extremist?

Joshua became known as one of the city's most outspoken voices for democracy. He challenged the government's right to make decisions without the people's support. But the government was unhappy about being challenged so publicly. It reacted harshly toward Joshua. China's government-run media labeled Joshua a dangerous **extremist**, although he still wasn't even old enough to drive a car.

? THINK ABOUT IT

Why was Joshua labeled as an extremist?

> *People should not be afraid of their government. The government should be afraid of their people.*
>
> —"Echoing Tiananmen, 17-year-old Hong Kong student prepares for democracy battle," CNN article, September 2014

Scholarism marched in the streets to challenge the government.

Reminders of the Past

For many people, the pro-democracy movement in Hong Kong was a reminder of student demonstrations that took place in China almost 25 years earlier. Joshua's father had taught him about the Chinese government's repression of demonstrations such as the Tiananmen Square protests. That protest was historic. It was large and showed students' willingness to challenge their government. It also displayed the Chinese government's willingness to push back with force.

Joshua (center) at a demonstration remembering victims of the 1989 Tiananmen Square crackdown by the Chinese government.

Tiananmen Square Protest

In 1989, Tiananmen Square in Beijing, China, was the site of massive student protests. They demanded democracy and human rights. Thousands of students took part in hunger strikes. The demonstration lasted for weeks and attracted more than one million protestors to Tiananmen Square. When the protestors ignored the government's pleas to end the demonstration, the army moved in. Many protestors were arrested and put in jail. Hundreds, and possibly thousands, were killed. No one knows for sure how many died. Stories of events such as this are strictly **censored** by the Chinese government.

Tiananmen Square

Tiananmen means "gate of heavenly peace."

The Occupy Movement

Soon after, Joshua and other protest leaders called on students to demonstrate again. They feared that their freedom was being threatened again by China's proposed changes to Hong Kong's voting system. Organizers called on protesters to block roads and occupy city squares in the heart of Hong Kong's busy financial district. They demanded that Hong Kong citizens be guaranteed freedom to select and vote for people of their choice to run Hong Kong.

People left messages of support for the protests on the walls of buildings.

A Leading Role

For 79 days, protestors occupied sites across Hong Kong, interrupting traffic and city services. In September, the demonstration ended with more than 70 people—including Joshua—arrested by police. He was released two days later. Joshua was becoming internationally recognized for the important role he played in organizing and participating in these demonstrations. But some people criticized his motives and accused him of plotting against China.

Yellow Umbrellas

The Occupy Movement was also known as the Umbrella Movement. Protestors used yellow umbrellas as a symbol of **resistance**.

Arrests and Discrimination

In the months that followed, Joshua often faced harassment. He was arrested briefly on several occasions for his role in the Umbrella Movement protests.

During one incident, he said he was beaten and insulted by police. In August 2015, Joshua and two other young leaders—Nathan Law and Alex Chow—were charged with organizing and attending an illegal protest during the 2014 demonstrations. They were ordered to perform **community service** as punishment.

No Entry

Joshua has even been denied entry into Malaysia and Thailand. It is thought that his political views are a threat to their countries' relations with China.

Hong Kong police arrest Joshua at a 2014 student protest.

Joshua introduces the Demosisto party at a press conference in 2016.

> "The future of Hong Kong should be decided by Hong Kongers.
>
> —**Joshua: Teenager vs. Superpower**, video, 2017"

A New Cause

In April 2016, Joshua and other Scholarism leaders formed a new political party called Demosisto. Their party's goal was to force the Hong Kong government to hold a **referendum** about the one party, two systems principle, which is to expire in 2047. They want to ensure that the rights and freedoms guaranteed to Hong Kong citizens under the principle will not be lost.

Actions and Consequences

Almost three years after the Umbrella Movement protests, the Hong Kong government decided the punishment of community service wasn't harsh enough. It decided instead to sentence Joshua, Nathan, and Alex to prison to make it difficult for them, and as a lesson to other protesters. News of their arrests sparked large protests. Joshua, who was now 20 years old, began a six-month prison sentence on August 17, 2017. He felt sorry for the worry his activism caused his parents.

? THINK ABOUT IT

Why did the government decide to sentence Joshua to prison instead of community service?

Unexpected Consequences

Joshua's parents have always encouraged his independent thinking and his commitment to standing up for what is right. But they never expected him to be sent to prison for his actions. Joshua had always carefully considered the **consequences** of his actions. Although he was not surprised by his community service sentence, he had not expected to be sent to prison.

" The government can lock up our bodies but they cannot lock up our minds.

— "Pro-democracy activists Joshua Wong and Nathan Law released from Hong Kong jail," CNN article, October 2017 "

Joshua and fellow activist Nathan Law (left) speak about their prison sentences for protesting.

Joshua's father Roger has supported and encouraged his son's activism.

Roger Wong

Joshua's father joked that strict prison rules taught his messy son to be tidy and organized.

Time to Reflect

While in prison, Joshua received letters of support from people around the world. These helped him stay positive while he received little other news about what was happening in the world outside. His **isolation** gave him time to reflect on his career as an activist. As he met other prisoners, Joshua listened to their stories and perspectives about society. He gained a deeper understanding of the issues faced by many Chinese citizens. More than ever, he was determined to fight for freedom and democracy.

A Triumphant Release

Joshua spent two months in prison before being released on October 24, 2017. More than 100 journalists were present to document the moment. Friends punched the air triumphantly to celebrate the news of his release. Supporters outside the courtroom held up yellow umbrellas as a sign of support. Joshua used his freedom to speak out. He encouraged people to remember other activists who remain in jail because they do not enjoy the same kind of international attention and support given to Joshua.

Cost of Freedom

Joshua's parents paid $50,000 Hong Kong dollars ($6,400 U.S.) to secure his release.

Time in prison made Joshua more committed to the ideals of free speech and democracy—even if he had to suffer.

Chapter 5

More Work to Do

Joshua believes there is still plenty of work to do in the fight for democracy. He is passionate about his city. He is determined that its citizens continue to enjoy the rights, freedoms, and independence they have been granted. Joshua has written a series of columns for the British newspaper, *The Guardian*. In those columns, he explained his activism. His role in the continued fight for democracy in Hong Kong is a strong example for others around the world.

> *I may have temporarily lost my freedom, but I have never regretted my involvement in the umbrella movement.*
>
> —Joshua Wong, "Prison is an inevitable part of Hong Kong's exhausting path to democracy," *The Guardian*

Awards and Recognition

Joshua is a remarkable young man who has encouraged ordinary citizens to demonstrate and fight for democracy. His courage and determination have been recognized with numerous awards.

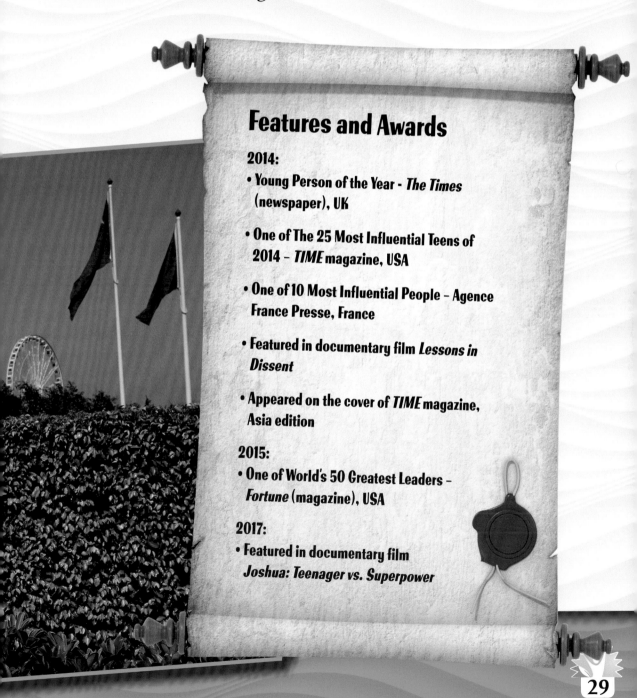

Features and Awards

2014:

- Young Person of the Year - *The Times* (newspaper), UK

- One of The 25 Most Influential Teens of 2014 – *TIME* magazine, USA

- One of 10 Most Influential People – Agence France Presse, France

- Featured in documentary film *Lessons in Dissent*

- Appeared on the cover of *TIME* magazine, Asia edition

2015:

- One of World's 50 Greatest Leaders – *Fortune* (magazine), USA

2017:

- Featured in documentary film *Joshua: Teenager vs. Superpower*

Writing Prompts

1. How did Joshua's father influence his decision to become an activist?

2. Do you think the Chinese government's accusation that Joshua is an extremist is fair? Why or why not?

3. What are some of the personal consequences Joshua has suffered as a result of his activism?

4. How were the Tiananmen Square protesters treated differently than the Umbrella Movement protesters?

5. What positive lessons did Joshua learn in prison?

Learning More

Books

This is Hong Kong: A Children's Classic by Miroslav Sasek. Universe, 2007.

Hong Kong by Falaq Magda. Cavendish Square, 2018.

The Tiananmen Square Massacre by Wil Mara. Scholastic, 2013.

Teenage Rebels: Stories of Successful High School Activists, From the Little Rock 9 to the Class of Tomorrow by Dawson Barrett. Microcosm, 2015.

Democracy by Sean Connolly. Hachette Kids Franklin Watts, 2017.

Umbrellas in Bloom: Hong Kong's occupy movement uncovered by Jason Y. Ng. Blacksmith Books, 2016.

Websites

www.amnesty.org/en/latest/campaigns/2017/09/hong-kong-dark-times-hope-people/
Four activists involved in the Umbrella Movement tell their stories.

www.accreditedschoolsonline.org/resources/student-activism-on-campus/
This website is dedicated to helping students become activists. Includes a six-step guide to becoming an activist and examples of causes activists can support.

Movies

Joshua: Teenager vs. Superpower
A 2017 documentary about Joshua Wong's movement designed to save his city.

Lessons in Dissent
A 2014 documentary, which follows Joshua Wong and Ma Jai, leading a generation of activists in Hong Kong. (Cantonese with English subtitles)

Glossary

activist A person who uses actions to help make changes in society

boycotts The refusal to buy, use, or participate in something as a protest

censored Removed ideas or stories that are considered offensive or harmful to society

civil disobedience The refusal to obey laws as a way of forcing the government to do or change something

Communist Based on the principles of Communism, which is a type of society organized so that products and industries are owned and controlled by the government rather than by individuals or companies

community service Work that is done without pay to help people in a community

consequences Something that happens because of someone's actions

curriculum The courses taught by a school

democracy A form of government in which people choose leaders by voting

elder A person who has authority because of age or experience

extremist Someone whose extreme ideas about politics or religion are considered dangerous

imprisonment The punishment of being kept in prison for a long period of time

inequalities Unfair situations in which some people have more rights than others

isolation The state of being in a place that is separate from everyone else

referendum An event in which people of a country vote on a law that deals with a special issue

repressed Forbid something from being said or done

resistance Refusal to accept or go along with something

sit-in A protest in which people stay in a certain place and refuse to leave until they are granted what they demand

social justice The equal distribution of rights and wealth between individuals in society

western Of or regarding the cultures of western Europe and North America

Index